The Queer

The Queer

An Interaction with the Gospel of John

Rev. Jeff Hood

WIPF & STOCK · Eugene, Oregon

THE QUEER
An Interaction with the Gospel of John

Copyright © 2016 Jeff Hood. All rights reserved. Except for brief quotations in critical publications or reviews, no part of this book may be reproduced in any manner without prior written permission from the publisher. Write: Permissions, Wipf and Stock Publishers, 199 W. 8th Ave., Suite 3, Eugene, OR 97401.

Wipf & Stock
An Imprint of Wipf and Stock Publishers
199 W. 8th Ave., Suite 3
Eugene, OR 97401

www.wipfandstock.com

PAPERBACK ISBN: 978-1-5326-1238-1
HARDCOVER ISBN: 978-1-5326-1240-4

Manufactured in the U.S.A.   NOVEMBER 29, 2016

For Rev. Dr. Stephen V. Sprinkle
who taught me the word.

The following is a recording of the queer events that took place when God visited North Texas...

Chapter 1

In the beginning was the Queer, and the Queer was with God, and the Queer was God. The Queer was there in the beginning with God. All things came into being through the Queer, and without the Queer not a single thing existed. Life flowed from the Queer and the Queer's life is the light of all people. The light shines in the darkness, and the darkness did not overcome it.

God sent a man to Texas named John as a witness to testify to the light, so that all might believe. John was not the Queer, but he came to testify to the light. The true Queer, who enlightens everyone, was coming to the world.

The Queer was in Texas already, Texas actually flowed out of the Queer, but

Texas was blinded. The Queer was rejected by the Queer's family and those who claimed to know God the best. But to all who received the Queer, who believed in the Queer's name, the Queer gave power to become children of God, born, not of blood, flesh, or will, but of God.

The Queer became flesh and dwelt among us here in Texas. We have seen the Queer's glory, the glory of a parent's only child, full of grace and truth. John screamed it out, "This is the Queer that ranks ahead of me because this Queer was here before me." From the fullness of the Queer we have all been showered with grace upon grace. Moses and our forefathers gave us the laws; grace and truth came through the Queer. No one has ever seen God. It is God the Queer, who is closest to God's heart, who has made God known.

The leaders of the Church of the Bible sent numerous pastors from Denton to ask John, "Who the hell are you? What the hell are you? What is your identification?" John confessed, "I aint the Queer. I aint the one sent by God to save you." Then they asked, "Well then, who the hell are you? Are you a pastor or priest? Are you Elijah?" John confessed, "I am not." "Are you a prophet?" He answered, "No." Then they asked, "Well then, who are you? Give us an identification, some type of label or something. What do you say for yourself?" John said, "I am the voice of the one crying out in the sticks, 'Make straight the way of the Queer,'" as the prophet Isaiah said many years ago.

Now these leaders were sent by their Senior Pastor, who was the head of the Church of the Bible in Denton. They wanted to maintain the doctrines and dogmas that kept the people in line. They questioned John, "Why are you baptizing if you are neither the one God sent to save us, nor Elijah, nor a prophet?" John answered, "I baptize with the waters of Lake Dallas. Among us stands one you don't know, I am not worthy to untie the shoes of the Queer who is coming." These events took place across the Loop near Lake Dallas.

The next day, as he was riding in a caravan of cars with his disciples right off of East University Drive, John saw the Queer walking. John demanded the caravan stop. Loudly, John declared, "Here is the Queer of God that takes away the sin of the world! This is the Queer we have been waiting for. This is the revelation I have been preaching. I saw the Spirit of God descend and remain on the Queer. God told me that I should follow the Queer who the Spirit of God descends and remains upon. God told me that this is the one who will baptize with the Holy Spirit. I have seen it. This is the Queer of God." The Queer was outed as the Queer in front of a caravan full of howling people on the side of the road.

The next day, not too far from Lake Dallas, John was hanging out with two of his disciples and the Queer slowly approached them. John outed the Queer again. "Look, it's the Queer of God!" The two disciples took notice and followed the Queer. When the Queer turned around and saw them, the Queer asked, "In this world of hatred, what are you looking for?" "Teacher, where are you staying?" The Queer invited them to come and see. It was a long walk over to Cooper Creek and the two were not used to walking. After they arrived, the disciples stayed and clung to the Queer. Later, Andrew, one of the two, went to get his brother and arriving exclaimed, "We have found the Queer!" Simon, Andrew's brother, rushed to meet this Queer. Immediately, the Queer changed Simon's name to Peter.

The next day, the Queer decided to go to Corinth. Arriving, the Queer saw Phillip and said, "Follow me." Now Phillip was from Shady Shores, the same little dot on the map as Andrew and Peter. Phillip found Nathanael and said to him, "We have found the one about whom Moses in the law and also the prophets wrote about, right over there, the Queer."

Nathanael responded, "Can anything good come from the trashy riffraff of Ponder?" Phillip said, "Come look for yourself." When the Queer saw Nathanael coming, the Queer declared, "Now, that right there, is an honest man." Nathanael asked, "Where do you know me from?" The Queer replied, "I was thinking about you sitting thinking under that street lamp." Nathanael replied, "My God! You are the Queer." To which the Queer replied, "You believe just because I pondered you sitting under a street lamp? You will see bigger, greater, more fantastical miracles than this... You will see heaven opened and the angels of God ascending and descending upon the Queer."

Chapter 2

On the third day, the Queer, the Queer's mother Mary, and the disciples of the Queer attended the wedding of a friend in Argyle. Later on in the evening, after everyone was fairly drunk, the wine gave out. "We don't have anymore wine," Mary loudly declared. The Queer replied, "Woman, why should I care? It aint my time yet." "Do what the Queer, that dark skinned person over there, says," Mary told the catering company. The Queer ordered six large plastic barrels, capable of holding twenty to thirty gallons of water, to be filled to the brim and said, "Now draw some water out and take it to the manager of your catering crew." The catering manager, tasting the substance, was shocked and could not figure out where the amazing wine came from.

"Everyone serves the best wine first and the cheap stuff after everyone gets drunk, why would you save the best wine until everyone is drunk?" the manager exclaimed to the groom. The Queer chose the wedding at Keller to perform the first of many miracles to come. The Queer was concerned with uplifting the joys of love. This queer event revealed the glory of the Queer and the mission of the Queer, love. The disciples believed.

Following the wedding at Argyle, the Queer went down to Highland Village for a rest with family and the disciples.

The high religious holidays were approaching, so the Queer went up to Denton. When the Queer arrived to the Church of the Bible, the Queer was mad as hell. Folks were everywhere oppressing people. They were scaring the shit out of people in order to get them to do what they wanted. Hell and damnation were on the tongues of everyone the Queer ran into. They had a homeless shelter that was only willing to help people if the folks got saved first, whatever the hell that means. They were telling people that God was an American and a Republican. They were sending people to reparative therapy, as if something is wrong with love. There was no justice or grace, only judgment of a world they knew nothing about. The word on everyone's lips was damnation. This self-described house of God was a house of exploitation and hate. The Queer could not take the hypocrisy and injustice of it all. Red with fury, the Queer fashioned a whip of chords and went to work. In a righteous anger, the Queer turned over the sound system, ripped down the projector, turned over the drums and guitars, tore down the American flag, demanded justice now, and declared to all that would listen that "God is love." To the pastors, the Queer exclaimed, "Get this hate and injustice out of here NOW! Stop using the name of God to create a marketplace of hate, oppression, and injustice!" The disciples remembered that it was written, "The Queer will be consumed by a zeal for the church and the people of God."

Some of the self-described religious folk were not fazed, "What proof can you give to us for doing all of this?" "Destroy all of this church and I will rebuild it in three days?" said the Queer. "How?" they demanded, "It took ten years to raise the money and five years to build." In the mind of the Queer, the temple was the body, not the Church of the Bible. After the Queer rose from the dead, following a hate crime fueled by religious violence, the disciples remembered that the Queer said that the Queer would be raised back up. The disciples believed in the resurrection of the Queer and the words of resurrection that the Queer had spoken.

In Denton, during this highly religious time, many believed in the Queer, because they saw the signs of the restoration. The blind were opening their eyes to sight. The Queer, however, did not trust the people enough to give them the Queer's body, because the Queer knew the destruction that people often inflict on the body and queerness already testifies for itself.

Chapter 3

Now one of the Church of the Bible pastors named Nicodemus, a prominent leader of the religious folk, heard the teachings of the Queer and was amazed. So he came to the Queer by night and said, "Teacher, I and many others know that you have come from God, for there is no way you could do all of these things unless you were from God." "Nicodemus, no one can see the Kingdom of God unless they are born from above," replied the Queer. Nicodemus was flummoxed, "How can anyone go back into their mother's womb and be born twice?" "You must be cleansed of the ways you think about yourself and the world. You must be reborn of water and the Spirit. What is born of flesh is flesh, and what is born of the Spirit is spirit. The wind blows where it chooses, and you hear the sound of it, but you don't know where it is coming from or where it is going. So is everyone who is born of the Spirit. Those who follow and practice love," declared the Queer. Nicodemus grew increasingly perplexed, having never thought of religion as anything but law and judgment, "How can it be so?" "You are a religious leader, and yet you don't understand what is really the way of God?" the Queer teased.

"Too often we speak to what we know and testify to what we have seen, yet fail to acknowledge and accept love in the process. You have difficulty acknowledging and accepting earthly things, how are you going to understand heavenly things? Look in front of you, no one has ascended to heaven except the one who actually descended from heaven, me, the Queer. Just as Moses raised the serpent in the sticks, so too must the Queer be raised up, that whoever believes in the Queer will have life eternal."

The Queer

"For God so loved the world that God gave God's only child, the Queer, so that whoever believes in the Queer will not perish but have life eternal."

"God did not send the Queer into the world to condemn the world, but in order to open the eyes of the world, that the world might be saved through the Queer. Those who believe in the Queer will not be condemned; but those who deny the Queer are condemned already, because they have not believed in love, which is God. And this is the judgment, light has come into the world, and people have loved the darkness of oppression, self-hate, and injustice because there was no love in their hearts. For all who do evil hate the light and do not come to the light, so their evil deeds won't be exposed. But those who love come to the light, so that their deeds might be proven to be love, God."

Later, the Queer and the disciples went into the countryside of unincorporated Denton County, when they arrived, there was extended fellowship and many baptisms in a small creek. At Lake Dallas, not too far from the Loop, John was baptizing those who kept coming to be baptized. One of the pastors from the Church of the Bible, snuck in amongst John's disciples and asked, "Why are more people going to the Queer to be baptized than are coming to you?" John replied, "I told you that I am not the Queer, I was merely sent to prepare the way for the Queer. I rejoice at the saving presence of the Queer. For this reason, 'The Queer must increase and I must decrease.'"

The one who comes from above is above all and the one from earth belongs to earth and speaks about earthly things. The Queer is above all. The Queer testifies to what the Queer has seen and heard, yet people are afraid of the queerness of the Queer. Whoever has accepted the testimony of the Queer, believes that God is truth and love. The Queer that God has sent speaks the words of God, for the Queer grants Spirit without hesitation.

The Queer

God loves God's child and has placed all things in the hands of the Queer. Whoever believes in the Queer has eternal life; whoever denies the Queer will not see life and must endure the pain of separation from God.

Chapter 4

Now when the Queer found out that the pastors of the Church of the Bible were discussing amongst themselves, how the Queer was making more disciples and baptizing more people than John, the Queer left rural unincorporated Denton County and headed toward the city of Argyle. Much to the dismay of the prejudices of the disciples, the Queer took a brief detour and traveled down into Dallas and stopped in the area called Oak Lawn. The Queer stopped and sat down right by a place that Jacob had given to his son Joseph, known as the Legacy of Love Monument. It was high noon and the Queer was about to confront the deeply held prejudices of many religious people.

The Queer

The Queer was alone, as the disciples had gone into the supermarket to buy food. While the Queer was sitting, a transgender person came to have a seat and drink a little bit of water out of a pack. The Queer looked up and said, "Could I have a small swig of your water?" The transgender person was baffled and surprised, "How is that you, a religious person, ask me for a drink, a transgender person of Dallas?" The Queer spoke to love and affirm the humanity of the person, "If you knew the gift of God, and who it is asking you for a drink, you would have asked me and I would have give you living water." The transgender person responded, "You don't have a cup for me to pour the water in and I didn't figure you wanted to drink after me. Where does this living water come from? Are you greater than our forbearers here in Oak Lawn, Jacob, his partners, and all his ancestors, who gave us this monument?" The Queer responded boldly and slowly, "Your monument is great, but it will only last for a time. Those who drink my water and trust in my love will never thirst again. The water and love I give is affirming and eternal, it gushes up to create the Kingdom of God." The transgender person excitingly said, "Please give me some of this water, this love, so that I may never again thirst."

"Go get your partner and come back," the Queer replied. "I have no partner," the transgender person said. "You are right. You have had five partners and the one you currently live with is not your partner." The transgender person was astonished and said, "You are indeed a prophet. Our ancestors have always worshipped here in Oak Lawn, but we are told that we must worship in the First Churches." The Queer knew the requirements for worship were unjust and responded, "Ma'am, believe me, the hour is coming where you can worship wherever you want. The hour is now here and approaching when true worshipers will worship the Queer in spirit and truth, for the Queer seeks true worshipers. The Queer God is spirit, and those who worship the Queer must worship in spirit and truth." The transgender person replied, "I know that the Queer is coming and when the Queer comes the Queer will reveal all things." The Queer didn't hesitate, "I am the Queer, the one whose voice you hear."

The disciples walked back up and brought their prejudices with them. The disciples were astonished that the Queer was speaking with a transgender person from Oak Lawn, but they dared not speak. The transgender person left everything and ran down Cedar Springs Road to the intersection with Throckmorton Street. Upon arrival, she yelled, "Come and see the Queer who just told me everything I have ever done! Could it be the Queer we have always longed for?" The people rushed to see.

During this time, the disciples urged the Queer to eat. The Queer said, "I have food to eat that you don't know about." The disciples replied, "Surely someone has not brought you food that we don't know about." The Queer pushed, "Loving the people of God and doing the will of the God who has sent me to complete God's work is the only sustenance I need. Stop looking around and saying that the harvest is four months away! The fields are ripe for the harvest right now. The Queer is already making a way to eternal life and inviting people into the Kingdom. You are a part of the plan. You are a part of the sowing, reaping, and spreading of love."

Large amounts of people in Oak Lawn believed in the Queer, due to the transgender person's testimony of "the Queer loved and told me everything about myself." When the Oak Lawnians talked to the Queer, they begged the Queer to stay for two more days. Throughout the time, people, one right after the other, just kept-on-believing in the Queer. They excitedly spoke to the transgender person, "Your testimony is what got us here, but now we have seen for ourselves and we know that this is the Queer, the Savior."

After two days, the Queer and the Queer's disciples headed toward Argyle. The Queer warned the disciples that the Queer is often not welcomed in the Queer's own home. Upon arrival, the Argylians welcomed the Queer; for they had seen all that the Queer had done in Denton.

Later, the Queer arrived in downtown Argyle, where the Queer turned the water into wine. Immediately, a Texas Ranger ran up to the Queer and asked the Queer to heal his son, who lay ill at the point of death in Justin. The Queer declared, "Unless you see signs and wonders many of you will not believe." The official pleaded, "Please, come before my young son dies." "Go and your son will live," the Queer responded. The man believed in the words of the Queer and headed to Justin. Somewhere around Northlake, the Texas Ranger's secretary met him and told him that his child was alive. The Ranger asked, "What time did he begin to get better?" "Yesterday at 1pm in the afternoon," the secretary responded. The Ranger realized that this was the exact time that the Queer said, "Your son will live." The Ranger and his entire household believed in the Queer. This was the Queer's second sign on the roads in incorporated and unincorporated Denton County.

Chapter 5

After this there was the Jazz Festival of Denton, and the Queer went up to Denton to check it out.

Once in Denton, the Queer traveled to the public pool off of Mingo Road. Scattered about were many sick people with nowhere else to go, including the blind, the lame, the paralyzed, the mentally ill, and many others. There was even a man who had been ill for over thirty-eight years. When the Queer saw the sick man the Queer inquired, "Do you want to get better?" The sick man answered, "I have no one to drop me into the pool when the angel of healing stirs the water. Someone always jumps in front of me." The Queer did not hesitate in response, "Stand up, take up your towel, and walk on out of here." At once, the sick man stood up and walked. The Queer did what the religious folk in Denton often refused to do, care about the healthcare of all people, including the least of these with dirty clothes and towels.

The day was Sunday and the religious folk in Denton had special rules about Sunday. Local religious folk told the formerly lame man, who was carrying a celebratory drink, "It is not lawful for you to carry alcohol on a Sunday morning." "The Queer who healed me told me to take up my towel, walk, and celebrate with a drink," replied the formerly lame man. Then the religious folk aggressively asked, "Where is the weird ass who told you all that? Where is this Queer?" "I don't know who, what, or where the Queer is, but I do know that I am healed," bluntly spoke the formerly lame man. Later, the Queer found the formerly lame man and declared, "You have been made well. You are a child of God. Act like it." The man went away and told the religious folk that the Queer from Ponder made him well. The religious folk did not like that the Queer was healing on the Sabbath and started to bully the Queer. But the Queer remained steadfast and responded, "My mother and father God is still working, and, as the child of God, I am also still working." For this reason the religious folk sought all the more to kill the Queer, not only was the Queer breaking the rules for Sunday, but the Queer was saying that God was the Queer's mother and father, thereby making the Queer equal to God."

The Queer said to them, "The child can do nothing alone, but is granted strength only when the child follows the ways of the parent; for whatever the parent does, the child does likewise. The parent loves the child and shows the child all that the parent is doing; and the parent will show greater works than these, so that all will be astonished. Indeed, just as the parent raises the dead and gives the dead life, so too does the child give life to whomever the child wishes. The parent of all judges no one and has given all authority for judgment to the child, so that all will honor the child just as they have honored the parent. Anyone who does not honor the child does not honor the God who sent the child. Honestly, anyone who hears these words and believes will have life eternal, they will pass from death to life. Honestly, the time is coming when the dead will hear the voice of the child, the very Queer of God, and those who hear will live. For just as the parent gives life, so to does the child give life, and has given the Queer to correct, because the Queer is God on earth. Do not be astonished. The hour is coming when all people in the graves will hear the voice of the Queer and spring forth to life. There will be eternal unrestricted love shown in the resurrection."

The Queer continued, "I can do nothing on my own. God grants all power to me and I seek to do God's will. Whatever I testify about the Queer is not true, but whatever God testifies about the Queer is true. John and his messengers told the truth as best they knew how. They pointed you to the truth of the Queer. John was a bright and shining lamp and for a while you got to dance in his light. But I bring a testimony that is greater than anything John ever said. I am the love of God. God's love testifies about me. If you don't believe in God, how could you hear such testimony? You look deep in the scriptures for eternal life, but eternal life is right in front of you. Come to me! If you do not have love in you, how could you have anything eternal in you? The Queer comes not to pursue the glory of humans, but, rather, to share the love of God. How come you are so desperate for glory on earth? Seek God's glory. Believe in the Queer. Believe in love. If you believe in Moses and all the prophets of the past, how can you not believe in me? Would you rather be judged by law or by the hope of grace? The prophets wrote about me. They told you that I was coming. If you haven't believe in love in the past, how can you believe in love when the Queer is right in front of your face?"

Chapter 6

After all this healing, loving, and teaching, the Queer decided to go to the other side of Lake Dallas, which at the southern tip is also occasionally called a rich folk's lake and at the northern tip a poorer folk's lake. A large crowd followed the Queer, some might have called it a traveling rainbow nation, along the muddy rocky shores of the lake. These folks had seen the signs of love and wanted to see more. The Queer went up on one of the steep grassy banks and sat down with the disciples. There were people everywhere, even some pulling up on boats. A religious festival was approaching. When the Queer saw the large crowd, the Queer told Philip, "Where are we going to buy food for all of these people?" This was a test. The Queer knew

The Queer

what was coming. Philip declared, "I could work six months and not have enough money to give all these people even a taste of food." Andrew, Simon Peter's brother, decided to try out his newfound faith and told the Queer, "Well, there is this boy here with five pieces of cornbread and two pieces of fried catfish." Backtracking a bit, Andrew added, "...but I guess that ain't much food in comparison to the appetites of all these folks." The Queer told the disciples, "Make everyone sit down." There was a bunch of green grass and everyone sat down. There were about five thousand colorful people sitting on a wide grassy plain next to Lake Dallas. Then Queer took the cornbread and the fried fish, blessed it, and started passing it out. When the crowd got done burping intermittently, the Queer told the disciples, "Gather up all the fragments that are left, we don't want to leave anything." When all the remnants were gathered back up, there were twelve large baskets left. The rainbow people were amazed and declared, "This is the prophet we have been looking for." The folks started to press in and wanted to elect the Queer to the United States Congress. Hearing this, the Queer quickly retreated and went up into the sticks to be left alone.

Around 8:00pm, unable to find the Queer, the disciples decided to take the boat out on Lake Dallas. They were going to go to the southern tip and eat near Highland Village. The sky began to darken, rain began to fall, lightening crashed, the wind increased, and the lake got really rough. The motor on the boat died and water began to fill up the interior. The disciples were in a bad way two or three miles from shore. Then, looking up, the disciples saw the Queer walking on water and coming toward the boat. The Queer's long hair and loose clothing were flowing in the storm. The disciples were terrified. The Queer looked up and declared, "It's me. Don't be afraid." When they took the Queer into the boat, they were immediately transported to Highland Village.

The next day, when the crowd saw that only one boat was taken. They knew that the Queer was not in the boat with the disciples and wondered where the Queer was. So when they couldn't find the Queer, they got into their boats to go to Highland Village. When they found the Queer, the people demanded, "How did you get here?" The Queer answered, "You are here because you are hungry. Do not work for food that perishes, but for the food that is eternal. The food that the Queer of God will give you." The people started to get bold and inquired, "How can we share in the work you are doing...showing the love and performing all the miracles?" The Queer declared, "The work of God is to believe in the Queer that God sent." That answer was not good enough for the people, who replied: "Well, what sign are you going to give so that we can know for sure? We want to see and believe. Where is the food from heaven you were talking about?" The Queer did not hesitate, "In the past, the bread from heaven you have received came from God. The bread of life is the power God uses to give life and light to all." The people begged, "Please give us this bread."

"I am the bread of life. Those who follow me will never be hungry or thirsty again. You are all witnesses, yet many of you don't believe. Everything that God gives me will come to me, and anyone who comes to me I will never turn away. I am from heaven. I come to do the will of God. I am not going to lose anything that God has granted me. I will raise up all things on the last day. This is the will of God, that all who see the Queer and believe in the Queer will have eternal life and I will raise them up."

The religious folk started complaining again. "How in the world could the Queer say 'I am the bread of heaven'?" "Is the Queer not the one they used to call the Queer of Ponder?" "How could the Queer have come down from heaven, we know that we was born to some trash out behind the public housing in Ponder?" The Queer, aware of their murmurings, replied, "Do not grumble. No one can know who the Queer is unless God grants sight. I give sight to the blind and it is those who see who will be raised up. Everyone who has heard the Queer has heard God. No one has seen God except for the one God sent, the Queer. Whoever believes lives forever. I know you are hungry, well I am the bread of life. Unlike earthly bread, this bread of the Queer is from heaven and those who eat it will never die. The bread I give for the life of the world is my flesh."

The religious folk just didn't get it, remarking, "How can the Queer ask us to eat the Queer's flesh?" The Queer replied, "Unless you eat the flesh and drink the blood of the Queer, you will not have eternal life. Those who do eat and drink, will be raised up. My body and my blood are true sustenance. Those who eat and drink abide in me and I in them. Whoever eats of me, eats of the living God. I am the bread of life that has come down from heaven. Ready to love and live forever?"

The Queer taught all of these things at the Church of the Village in Highland Village.

Many of the disciples were flummoxed by these teachings and wondered aloud, "So, is this about cannibalism? How can we accept this?" The Queer whipped around and inquired, "Does this teaching offend you? What if you actually saw the Queer ascending and descending to and from heaven? It is the spirit that gives life. The flesh is useless. My words are life. But among you there are many who don't believe." The Queer knew who would follow the Queer's teachings and who would remain closeted. The Queer loudly declared, "Those come after me are sent by God."

Hundreds of disciples turned back to the closet, marched in, and slammed the door. They were unable to handle the freedom and love that the Queer was offering. Finally, the Queer looked to the twelve and blurted out, "Are you going to?" Simon Peter spoke up, "Queer, where else shall we go? You alone have the words that make us free. I am not going back to that closet. We believe that you are the God who offers true freedom. We know that you are the Queer that God has sent to save us." The Queer replied, "I chose you twelve, yet one of you will hand me over to a bloodthirsty homophobic mob." The Queer was speaking of Judas.

Chapter 7

The Queer decided to go to Corinth. The Queer was scared to go into Denton, as the religious folks and the leadership at the Church of the Bible were tired of the Queer's queerness and words, they were ready to kill the Queer and looking for an opportunity. One of the religious festivals was approaching. The Queer's brothers taunted the Queer and said, "Why don't you come out and go on up to Denton for the festival? Why are you trembling scared in the closet? If you really are the Queer, then let everyone see your queerness. If you are so confident in yourself, show the world who you really are." The Queer's brothers didn't believe. The Queer replied, "It is not my time yet, but your time of privilege is always here. The world doesn't hate you, but it hates me because of my queerness and the fact that I shine light on the stifling injustices of the world. Go to the festival yourselves. I am not going. They are not ready for the coming of the Queer and my time has not yet come." The Queer remained in Corinth.

Unable to sit still, the Queer decided to go up to Denton for the religious festival in drag, so that no one would recognize the Queer. The religious folk and all the leaders of the Church of the Bible were looking for the Queer. In all actuality, the Queer was the talk of the festival. "Where is the Queer?" As the Queer walked around, the Queer consistently heard murmurs, "The Queer is a good person;" "The Queer is a false prophet;" or "The Queer is a liar." No one would speak to loud for fear of all the religious folks.

About halfway through the festival, the Queer began to teach in drag from the pulpit at the Church of the Bible. The religious folks were astonished. "How does a drag queen have so much knowledge with no seminary education?" The Queer answered directly, "My teaching is from the God who sent me. Anyone who is connected to God knows that I am the Queer sent by God. Those who speak apart from God seek their own glory. I seek the glory of the God who sent me. There is nothing false in my God."

"All of you are so religious, yet none of you exhibits the love and compassion of God. Right now, as we speak, you want to drag me out of here and make me another hate crime statistic." The religious crowd snapped back, "You are possessed to be talking about God and dressed in drag. You disgust us." The Queer replied, "You are the ones who are astonished by my teachings. You are the ones clamoring for miracles. You use me for a show to get off on and then want to toss me away. You know much about the law, but little about love. I am healing people who are sick and loving those you care nothing about. If you have not love, you have not God.

You should stop judging based on appearances and assumptions, but judge based on the love that is in the heart."

Many of the folks of Denton kept saying, "Isn't that the Queer the religious folks are trying to kill? And there the Queer is, in drag, speaking openly and freely. Could it be that some might actually believe that this is the Queer sent to open their eyes to love and offer them salvation from their prejudiced condemning hearts?" The Queer knew what they were saying and could not hold back any longer, "You know who I am. You know where I am from. Unfortunately, you have turned your backs on God and all the people who are queer around you. God is love and love opens our eyes to what is truly in front of us. I am the Queer and I know the Queer who sent me." Then the pastors from the Church of the Bible tried to have the Queer arrested as the Queer left the pulpit. It was as if there was a forcefield around the Queer, because none of the officers could touch the Queer. The hour had not yet arrived. Many in the crowd believed the Queer's words, yet some kept saying, "When God really does come in human form, do you really think God will be in drag?

The pastors of the Church of the Bible were furious and got together with other religious folk to demand that the Denton police arrest the Queer. To which the Queer replied, "I am going to be with you a little while longer, and then I am going back to God. You will search your hardest and not be able to find me. Where I am going you cannot go in your current evil states." The pastors looked at each other and said, "Where does the Queer intend to go? Does the Queer intend to go up to Oklahoma? What is the Queer talking about with this 'you wont be able to find me stuff'? We will go anywhere to end this poisonous queer behavior. We have had it!"

On the last day of the festival, the Queer cried out, "All who are thirsty come to me. Let the one who believes in me drink and never thirst again. Out of the followers of the Queer will flow living water that will bring life and wash away hate and injustice in the world." The Queer was talking about the living water of the Spirit of God. The water was coming.

When many of Dentonites heard these words, they started declaring, "This really is the Queer we have always waited for. This is the prophet of love, hope, and salvation." Still others couldn't believe and responded, "Surely God does not come from Ponder? Surely God was not born behind public housing? Surely God was not born into such a trashy family?" There was great division in the crowd concerning the Queer. The pastors of the Church of the Bible still wanted the Queer arrested, but no one laid hands on the Queer.

The Denton police reported back to the Church of the Bible, who asked, "Why didn't you arrest that disgusting queer?" To which the Denton police replied, "Never has anyone spoken like this!"

The pastors at the Church of the Bible couldn't stand it, "Surely you have not decided that God is the Queer in drag? Have you been bamboozled too? Have any of our pastors or any religious folk been deceived into believing this shit?" Nicodemus, who was a pastor at the Church of the Bible and friends with the Queer, replied "Do we not live in a society where the law says that people are innocent until proven guilty? You homophobes are trying to kill the Queer by mob violence and hate crime. Do you not understand the hate that is driving you?" The pastors snapped back, "Prophets don't come from Ponder. God is not a bastard piece of trash that proceeded out of a promiscuous mother. Ponder has never produced anything worth calling even remotely religious, much less produced the child of God. Nicodemus needs his head examined. God comes in drag?"

Chapter 8

The Queer went up on a bluff right outside of Denton to pray. Before light, the Queer started to walk toward the Church of the Bible to pray. All of the members of the church and some folks from the community all came to see the Queer and the Queer began to teach. Suddenly, the doors busted open and the pastors of the Church of the Bible drug in a woman caught in an adulterous relationship. She was forced to stand in front of the pastors. "This woman was caught in the act of adultery. Based on our laws, we have got to kick her out of the church, shun her from the community, and treat her as if she is dead. What do you say?" This was a test of the extent of the love of the Queer. Instead of answering, the Queer stooped down and used a marker to start writing on the floor tile all the names of the men and women the pastors at the Church of the Bible masturbated to, the men and women besides their wives that the pastors had engaged in intercourse with, and many other secret things. The Queer then spoke, "Let any of you misogynists who are without sin cast the first stone." The Queer stooped down and started writing some more. The pastors tucked their tails and got out of the church as quickly as possible. The Queer, now alone with the woman, beckoned, "Where are your misogynistic accusers? "They are gone and no one accuses me anymore," replied the woman. "Nor do I. Go and love the right way."

The Queer declared, "I am the light of the world. Those who follow me will never walk in darkness but will have the light of life." The pastors of the Church of the Bible responded in a fury, "How can anyone say such things about their self? This is ludicrous. You cannot prophecy about yourself!" The Queer slowly

The Queer

responded, "I am the Queer. My testimony is valid because I know who I am and where I am going. You do not. You judge everyone using human measurements. I judge no one. If I did judge, I would judge based on God. Your law says that you need two witnesses. I and God are two in one. I and God testify to who I am." "So, where exactly is God?" they inquired. "You don't know me and you don't know God. If you knew me you would know God," the Queer replied. The Queer spoke these words in the vestibule of the Church of the Bible. No one arrested the Queer. The hour was not yet right.

"I am going leave you and you won't find me. You will die in your hateful oppression. Where I am headed, you can't come," the Queer shared. The baffled religious folk responded, "Is the Queer going to commit suicide or something?" "You are from down here, I am from up there; You are from this world, I am not. You will die in your sins without me," the Queer replied. They all were still befuddled and said,

"Who the hell are you?" The Queer, frustrated, replied, "Why do I even speak to you? There is much to say and condemn about all of you. Today, all I do is declare what I have heard from God." Those present just didn't get it. Their minds were stuck in a normative way of thinking and they could not comprehend the queerness of the message. The Queer sought to clarify, "You won't realize who I am until I am murdered. You will then know that I am the child of God, the Queer, who is given authority and voice by God. God is with me. God will not leave me. I live to follow God." Many of those who heard began the process of belief.

Then the Queer said to the religious folk who started to believe, "If you follow the Queer then you are my disciples. When you follow the Queer, you will know the truth and the truth will set you free." Some of the other people answered, "We are Americans and have always been free. What are you talking about freedom?" The Queer did not hesitate, "Everyone who keeps on doing the same evil over and over is a slave to evil. Do you want to be a slave to evil? If the Queer makes you free, if you are able to accept who you were created to be, you will be truly free. As long as you chase after normativity you will be a slave to normativity. Be free! You want to kill me, because I want to destroy your materialistic normative society. In the Kingdom of God the last are first. What are you doing chasing normativity? Love God and love yourself! You are hearing the freeing words of God right now. Queer or not, you should listen."

The skeptics still barked, "We are Americans. Descended from the founding fathers. We are freedom loving people!" The Queer said to them, "Your love for America blinds you to what is standing in front of you. You are trying to kill me, the Queer, a messenger of the truth of God, because your values have blinded you to truth. You care about America more than you do your neighbors." They replied, "Our freedoms have been paid for with blood, sweat, and tears. We are the moral compass of the world not you!" The Queer demurred, "If your first priority was God, then you would love me, the Queer. I have come from God. In fact, God is standing right in front of you. God sent me to declare true freedom. Why are you so afraid of queerness? Is it because you cannot accept the way that I look, act, or love? Your bigotries and prejudices make you closer akin to the devil. From the beginning, the devil has been the source of oppression, injustice, homophobia, and bigotry. The devil pushes others to join in on these evils. Is that where you are? I tell the truth and whoever does not believe in me has fallen victim to the lies of the devil. How long will you allow constructs like American, straight, privileged, and others hold you back from loving God, yourself, and your neighbors? Stop with the normativity and injustices. Follow me! If you are from God you will hear the words of God. Those who cannot hear the words of the Queer are not from God."

The religious folk got very angry at these words. "You are a lesbian and you have a demon!" The Queer answered, "I do not have a demon. I honor God and you dishonor me. I am not here for myself. I am here for you. God alone gets the glory. Those who learn to become queer as I have will live forever." The religious folk were ready to battle at the sound of such perceived apostasy, "You are a demon. All of the greatest people to ever live died. How can you say, 'Whoever follows you and learns to be queer will never taste death?' Are you greater than George Washington, Abraham Lincoln, John Kennedy, or Ronald Reagan? They all died. Who the hell do you think you are?" The Queer responded loudly, "God queered me. God sent me. God loves me. You claim God but spout oppression and hate. What do you know about love? If I said I don't know love or God then I would be a liar like all of you. Don't claim to be welcoming if you don't really mean it. Your American heroes have waited for my arrival to restore justice to the world. I have seen them. I have talked to them. The entire world has waited patiently on the Queer and I am here." The religious folk were livid, "You are young. How could you have met all of these heroes who have died?" The Queer stood straight and replied, "Before Ronald Reagan was, I am." Folks in Texas like Ronald Reagan a lot, thus the religious folk picked up stones to kill the Queer. The Queer ran out of the Church of the Bible and hid behind the railroad tracks.

Chapter 9

The Queer was walking downtown on the square and saw a man who was blind. The disciples asked, "Whose fault is it that this man is blind, who sinned to cause it, the man or his parents?" The Queer responded, "Nobody sinned. The man was born blind so that God might be revealed through him. While it is still day I must do the works of the God who sent me, for night is coming when nobody can work. As long as the Queer is in the world, the Queer is the light of the world." The Queer hawked a loogie into a bed of flowers and made mud with the dirt. The Queer placed the concoction into the blind man's eyes and told him to go and wash his eyes in the pubic water fountain on the westside of the square. The blind man did as he was told and was able to see. All of those on the square and those who knew the blind man simply could not believe he could now see. "Isn't this the guy who annoyed us incessantly trying to get across the street and asking for money?" Some said, "Yep, that's him." Others said, "Nope that just looks like him." The formerly blind man screamed, "It is me!" The people wouldn't listen, because they didn't think he had the socioeconomic standing to be trusted. This was far to queer for most of the gathered, "How can someone be blind and then they see?" The minds and hearts of the gathered were too attuned to normativity to see. They were the ones that were blind. The Queer was giving sight to those who accepted the queerness of binding life to the Queer. The formerly blind man tried again, "The Queer made mud from a bed of flowers, spread it in my eyes, and told me to go wash my eyes in the water fountain on the westside of the square. I went, I washed, and now I see." "So where is this Queer now?" they inquired. "I don't know," replied the formerly blind man.

Not too long after, people brought the man who had formerly been blind to the pastors at the Church of the Bible. It was Sunday and the church was very busy. The pastors asked, "How did you get your sight back son?" "The Queer put mud pies on my eyes, I washed the mud pies off, and now I see," replied the man quite clearly. The pastors roared back, "The Queer cannot be from God, because the Queer doesn't heal through the church. The Queer doesn't follow the values and norms of the church. This is sin. How can a sinner perform such tasks?" The pastors were divided. They didn't know how to respond. "What do you say?" they asked the formerly blind man. "I think the Queer is of God."

The religious folk called the formerly blind man a liar and many refused to believe he had ever been blind. So, they decided to call his parents. His parents timidly replied, "Our son was blind. We don't know how he can now see. Ask him. He can answer for himself." There were a lot of powerful people who went to the Church of the Bible and were rabidly religious in Denton, the parents were afraid to answer the questions directly. The Church of the Bible had already agreed that anyone who believed the Queer to be God would be thrown out of the community. The parents were relieved when they stopped pestering them.

The religious folks confronted the formerly blind man and said, "Give glory to God and answer these questions truthfully. The Queer is a disgusting vile sinner. Do you know what people like the Queer do?" "I don't care what the Queer does. I only know one thing. I once was blind, now I see," he retorted. "What happened to you? How did this happen?" they kept pestering. "I have told you. You will not listen. Are you curious to hear it again because you want to become the Queer's disciples?" the formerly blind man replied. The religious folks were pissed, "You are the Queer's disciple! You are disgusting as the Queer is! You don't fit in because you are evil!

Where does this Queer come from?" The man replied, "I can see. My eyes were closed and now they are open. Healing comes from God, how could the Queer not be from God? Such a miracle has never happened before. This is God. Those who are not from God can do nothing." They couldn't take it anymore and the people drove the man out of Denton, screaming, "You evil man! What makes you think you have a damn thing to teach us?"

The Queer heard what happened and went out to find the formerly blind man hiding out past the Loop, "Do you believe in the Queer of God?" "Maybe, who is it? Tell me, so that I might believe..." the man replied. "The Queer is speaking in front of you right now," affirmed the Queer. "My Lord, My God, I believe," joyfully shouted the man. The Queer stepped further, "I came into the world, specifically, Texas, to push those who are blind so that they might see and to tell those who think they see, that they are blind." One of the pastors of the Church of the Bible had followed the Queer and loudly spoke up, "Are we the blind ones you speak of?" "You tell the world how to see yet you are blind," replied the Queer.

Chapter 10

"You cannot enter the fold but through love. The one who opens the gate and leads the fold is named love. When love calls the fold by name, they come and follow because they know the voice of love. Those who love will not run to evil, but will follow me." The Queer used this phrasing, but nobody got it.

The Queer tried again, "I am love. Everyone else is trying to do things partially, don't follow them. Follow love, for I am love. Whoever embraces love, will find rest for their weary searching. Evil comes only to steal, kill, and destroy. The Queer has come that you all might enjoy love and life in abundance."

"I am the lover. The lover always lays down the lover's life for the beloved.

Partial loves run away and leave the beloved, where the beloved gets wounded and destroyed. Those who are partial do not care entirely, only partially. I am the full lover. I know my beloved and my beloved know me. God knows me and I know God. I lay down my life for the beloved. My beloved are all over, in many different folds. I will call all of them to love and they will listen. I will call for love to exist in one flock as one people as one love. I am the shepherd, love. I lay down my life for love and God will take it up again. Love never dies. No one takes my life, I lay it down for love. I have the power to lay it down and take it right back up. God grants such power to God."

The heads on the religious folks were spinning. They argued amongst themselves on how best to respond. Some said, "The Queer is possessed!" Others said, "How can someone who speaks so beautifully of love and who opens the eyes of the blind be possessed?"

Later, around late winter, at the Festival of the 35 in Denton, the Queer was hanging out with friends. A few of the religious folks saw the Queer dancing and cornered the Queer, "Tell us the truth! Are you the Messiah?" The Queer replied, "I have told you who I am and you don't believe. The miracles I have done don't speak loudly enough? You do not care about truly seeing. Those who seek to love hear my voice and know who I am. I give them love eternal and they, like love, will never die. No one will take my beloved from me. I will pursue all of them to the ends of time and space. No one can snatch my beloved away from God. God and I are one."

The religious folks started to pull out knives, guns, and broken bottles to harm the Queer. "I have loved you, caused the lame to walk, and opened the eyes of the blind. You are going to stone me for this?" retorted the Queer. They shot back, "You are a blasphemer. You are only human yet you call yourself God." The Queer slowly and methodically replied, "Do you not believe that we are all children of God? Then, why do you call it blasphemy when I say I am the child of God? God sent me into the world. If I am working in love and healing, then don't believe me, just believe the works. If you believe the works, you believe in me. If you believe in love, you believe in me. If you believe in hope, you believe in me. These entities exist so that you might know the source, God. I am love. I am hope. I am the child of God and I and parent are one. If you don't believe in love or hope or healing then don't believe in me." The religious folks were beside themselves once more and they were going to kill the Queer, a hate crime was brewing, but the Queer escaped from their hands.

The Queer ran away across the Loop and out to Lake Dallas. Pitching a tent on the shore, the Queer remained hidden in the woods for a time. Many came out to the Queer. People consistently said, "John didn't do any of these miracles, but everything John said about the Queer was true." Many believed in the Queer and found love to be supreme.

Chapter 11

Now a certain man had the AIDS virus, Lazarus of Krum, the small town of Mary and Martha. Mary was the one who would pour out her perfume on the Queer and sensually rub it in with her hair. Lazarus, Mary's brother, had been experiencing complications with the AIDS virus for quite some time. The sisters called for the Queer to hurry to Krum, "the man with whom you have shared love is ill." When the Queer heard the message the Queer responded, "The AIDS virus does not lead to death. I am about to show up and show out." Though the Queer deeply loved Martha, Mary, and Lazarus, the Queer rested for two more days in Keller.

When the Queer suggested that it was time to go to Krum. The disciples begged the Queer not to go that close to Denton, "Pastor, the Church of the Bible and all the religious folk want to stone all of us, please don't take us there!" The Queer said, "There is still daylight. I am the light of the world. Night is coming. Then for a time there will be reason to fear." After these statements the Queer declared, "Our friend Lazarus has fallen asleep, but I am going to get him up." The disciples replied, "If Lazarus has just fallen asleep, he will be easy to wake up." The Queer, however, meant that Lazarus was dead. Then the Queer made it plain for them, "Lazarus is dead. You will see him rise and believe. Let's go to him." Thomas looked around and declared to all the disciples, "We might as well go and die up there in Denton with the Queer."

When the Queer arrived, the Queer found out that Lazarus had been dead for four days. Now Krum was very close to Denton, less than a couple miles, and many of the religious folk that harassed the Queer earlier were there to console Mary and Martha. When Martha found out that the Queer was coming, she ran to the end of the long driveway to meet the Queer, Mary stayed in the house. Martha cried out to the Queer, "If only you had been here, my brother would not have died. But, I know that God will give you whatever you desire." The Queer shouted, "Your brother will live again!" Martha replied, "I know that you will raise him up on the last day into your Kingdom of Love." The Queer said, "I am the resurrection and the life. Those who believe in me will never die. Do you believe this?" She replied, "You are the Queer, the Messiah sent to save the world, the child of God."

When Martha heard these things, she ran back to get her sister Mary, and told her, "Hurry, the pastor of all pastors is here and calling you." When Mary heard that the Queer wanted her, she got up and quickly went to the Queer. The religious folk who were at the house to console, with phrasing like "It was God's will," "This must have been his time," and

"God must have needed another angel," saw Mary get up rapidly and, concerned for her mental state, chased after her. The Queer was still at the end of the driveway milling around. When Mary got to the Queer, she hit the floor and declared, "My God, if you would have been here, my brother wouldn't have died!" When the Queer saw the deep emotion and tears, the Queer was overcome and deeply moved, "Where is he?" "Come look," they replied. The Queer wept. The religious folk could see the emotion flowing out of the Queer and declared, "The Queer must have been partnered with Lazarus." Other religious folks grumbled, "If the Queer is so special, and was probably partnered with him, then why couldn't the Queer have kept him from dying?"

When the Queer arrived at the grave, the Queer said, "Dig him up!" Everyone was shocked and Martha said, "Lord, Lazarus has been in there for four days." "If you believe, you will see you God," the Queer replied. So, they dug. When they arrived at the casket, they unlatched the lid and stood back. "God, AIDS has no power when I show up, I thank you for having heard me," the Queer professed for the sake of all who were there and all who would read this account. The Queer cried out with a loud voice, "Lazarus get up out of there and come embrace me!" The dead man came out, working out the embalming solutions as he regained motion, and embraced the Queer. After a moment, the Queer said, "By the power of the Queer, you are free to live and love whoever you want."

Many of the religious folk, who saw what actually happened, were shocked and believed on the spot. But some of them went to the pastors at the Church of the Bible and told them what the Queer did. So the Senior Pastor called together a meeting of the leadership of the Church of the Bible and declared, "We must do something now! The Queer is taking away part of our membership, donations are down, and the Queer's message of love is superseding our message of judgment and rules. The signs, however the Queer is doing them, is giving credence to the Queer's message. If we let the Queer continue we will lose our church, our political control, and our stranglehold on the values of our nation. I know what we must do, for it is better for the Queer to die than to lose everything we have worked so hard to attain. The Queer must die so that the people might be saved and brought back together." From that day forward, the Church of the Bible planned to kill the Queer.

The Queer did not walk or talk openly for a time at the Church of the Bible or amongst the religious folk, but went far away to Meunster in the region close to Oklahoma and remained there with the disciples.

Now the great religious Festival of the Spring was approaching and many from the region went to Denton to participate in plays of passion at the Church of the Bible, the Senior Pastor and all of the subordinate pastors were looking for the

Queer. The religious folk of Denton were on the look out for the Queer and saying, "Surely, the Queer will not come to the festival or any of the plays of passion?" The Church of the Bible gave orders that any person who saw the Queer should arrest the Queer immediately and bring the Queer to the church leadership.

Chapter 12

Six days before the Festival, the Queer rode down to Krum, the home of the risen Lazarus. There was a feast. The Queer ate heartily. Martha served and Lazarus sat at the table. Sensing that she had a more important duty, Mary took a bottle of the most expensive perfume she could find, Rubies. Mary took her Rubies and poured them on the Queer's feet. She loved the Queer. There was something incredibly sensual and moving about the act. Such feelings only increased when Mary took her hair and rubbed the perfume in with broad strokes. The house was filled with a beautiful tangible scent. Everyone loved the moment except Judas Iscariot, "What type of queen allows this type of activity? That perfume could have been sold for 30,000 dollars! We could have fed all the poor in Denton!" The other disciples thought that it was funny that Judas was saying such things because they had suspected him for some time of taking his own cuts out of what he called "the queen's purse." The Queer snapped the Queer's head back and shook the Queer's finger, "Leave Mary alone. This is about anointing my body for my burial. The poor will always need your help, but you will not always have my body to anoint."

When the religious folks learned that the Queer was in Krum, they came to see both the Queer and the risen Lazarus. The Senior Pastor and the staff of the Church of the Bible decided that Lazarus needed to be put to death as well, to hide the evidence of his resurrection, as many folks were leaving the church and believing in the Queer.

The next day, a huge crowd at the Festival of Spring heard that the Queer was coming into Denton. So they took rainbow flags and ran out to meet the Queer.

When they arrived at the road that the Queer was walking in on they shouted, "Hallelujah! Blessed is the Queer who comes in the name of God. Hallelujah! This is the Lesbian of all Nations!" The Queer found a longhorn and rode it into Denton. The Queer knew that it was previously written, "Do not be afraid, people of faith, your Queen is coming, sitting on a longhorn's back." The disciples did not realize what was going on, between the multitude of rainbow flags waving and the Queer on the back of the longhorn there was much to be distracted by. These events were prophesied to take place before the glorification of the Queer. The crowd continued to testify, shout, and sing about the miracle of Lazarus' resurrection in Krum. The Queer was a celebrity. The pastors of the Church of the Bible took notice, "The Queer is a fucking celebrity. The world wants to know that transgender asshole. We must eliminate the Queer now!"

Now there were some folks from Massachusetts visiting the Festival of Spring.

They approached Phillip and declared, "We have got to meet the Queer!" Phillip took Andrew with him to go tell the Queer of the folks from Massachusetts. The Queer replied, "The hour has come for the Queer to be glorified and made a celebrity. When grain dies it bears much fruit. Those who cling to life will lose it, but those who let go will gain eternity. If you want to know me then follow me. Be where I am. Whoever does this, God will honor."

"I am troubled in my soul. Should I do what I am supposed to do or should I ask God to save me? No, this is my destiny. God, I follow you," agonized and theorized the Queer. Then a soft tender feminine voice came from heaven, "I love you. I ordain it. I glorify it. Go my child." The crowd that heard the voice coming from heaven couldn't believe it. Some doubted and said, "It must have been a jet engine overhead." Others believed and said, "It was an angel speaking to the Queer." The Queer explained things, "The voice has come for you not me. The judgment of the world is coming. Evil will be driven out. When I am raised up, I will draw all people unto me." The people sensed that the Queer thought that the Queer would be experiencing a violent death soon. "We thought that the Messiah was supposed to remain with us forever? How can you say you are Messiah and that you must be raised up? Who is this Child of God? Is it you?" The Queer replied, "The light will only be with you for a little longer. Walk while you have the light, so you can see where you are going, for night is coming. Believe in the light. Become children of light."

After the Queer said these words, the Queer ducked into a gay bar and hid. The Queer was wise enough to know that the pastors of the Church of the Bible wouldn't follow the Queer into a place where there was alcohol and queer folk. Although the Queer loved them and performed many signs in their presence, they still didn't believe. They couldn't. They loved privilege too much. This fulfilled the words of Isaiah, "No one has believed our message. No one has believed God." and "Their eyes are blinded and hearts hardened. If they will turn their eyes and hearts to God, they will be healed." Isaiah knew what was coming. Nevertheless, though they knew these words and saw the miracles, the religious folk and the pastors of the Church of the Bible refused to believe in the miracle of God's love manifested before them. Others believed, unable to deny what they felt and what they saw, but were scared to speak publicly. The pastors of the Church of the Bible were on the prowl and declared that they would put anyone out of the community who believed in the Queer. The pastors simply loved their privilege more than God.

Then the Queer cried aloud: "Whoever believes in the Queer is believing in the God who sent the Queer. Whoever sees this lesbian sees the lesbian in the sky. The Queer has come to set this world on fire with love, inclusivity, and hope. Everyone who believes in me does not have to walk in the evils of injustice and oppression any longer. I am not here to judge. I am here to save...the world. The ones who reject me as weird and nonnormative rejects God as weird and nonnormative. For I am not speaking on my own, I am speaking on behalf of a God that is queer and loves the entirety of people in the world. This God rejects the religiosity you have created based on who is in and who is out. The God who is queer desires eternal life for all people in all places."

Chapter 13

Now right before the Festival of the Spring, the Queer knew that the Queer's hour of death was fastly approaching and that God was waiting. There was just too much hate bubbling all over the town. The Queer loves all people, because they are all the people of the Queer. The Queer was ready to love them to the end. The evil was already moving in the heart of Judas Iscariot. During the Festival of Spring celebratory supper at the house of a sympathetic supporter, the Queer, knowing that the entire world belonged to the Queer, got up from the table and filled a basin full of water. Whipping a towel around the Queer's hips, the Queer began to wash the feet of all of the disciples. Never before had God personally washed the feet of every sexuality, identity, ability, and race under one roof. When the time came to wash Peter's feet, Peter asked, "Lord, you really think you are going to wash my feet?" The Queer replied, "You will understand all of this one day." Peter couldn't understand and said, "You are never going to wash my feet I am too wounded and dirty." The Queer grew frustrated and replied "Unless I wash you, you will not share with me." Peter relented, "Ok, if you are going to wash my feet then wash everything." The Queer was growing tired of the back and forth, "One who is clean does not need to wash anything but the feet, for the feet have been walking. All of you are clean, but one has dirty hands."

After the Queer washed all of the feet, put the Queer's outer clothes back on, and returned to the table, the Queer said, "Do you know what just happened? You call me the professor, the pastor, and the Lord...you are right, this is what I am. So, if I humble myself to wash people's feet shouldn't you also? I have set an example. Serve people. Remember the example of God. I have chosen you. This is to fulfill scripture. There is one who will betray me. I tell you this so that you will know who and whose I am when these events transpire. Whoever receives one of my children receives me and whoever receives me receives the God who sent me."

After saying all of these things over supper, the Queer became very troubled, "One of you is going to betray me." The disciples looked at each and didn't know what to say. John, the disciple that the Queer loved, was reclining on the Queer and Peter motioned for him to ask the Queer who the Queer was talking about. John leaned over and whispered in the Queer's ear, "Who is it?" The Queer answered, "It is the one that I give this piece of pita to after dipping it in the hummus." The Queer gave the bread to Judas. After being embarrassed, an evil rage entered Judas and he raced out. The Queer told him as he passed, "Do what you have to do quickly." No one at the table knew what was going on. They just thought it was a little drama. Some thought that Judas was mad because he had to go buy some more food or perhaps that the Queer asked him to give more money to the poor. It was very dark.

When Judas left, the Queer said, "I am straight, but I have been glorified with queerness. The very queerness of being glorified by God. God is in me, God will glorify God's self, and will glorify God at once. Little ones, I am here for just a little bit longer. You will look for me and not be able to find me. Where I am going you cannot come right now. The greatest commandment is to love all of one another without qualification. Just as I have loved all of you. Follow me. Everyone will know that you are follows of the Queer, if you love one another."

Peter couldn't take it anymore, "Lord where are you going?" The Queer replied, "Where I am going right now you cannot come, you will follow later." Peter said, "I want to go where you go. I will lay my body down for you." The Queer answered, "Before the dog barks three times you will deny me."

Chapter 14

"Don't be scared. Believe in God, believe in me. God has prepared a place that is amazing for all of us. There is room for all of you. Would I lie to you? One day, you will join me. You know the directions." Thomas was flustered, "We don't know the directions. How could we?" The Queer in a powerful voice said, "I am the way, I am the truth, and I am the life. No one comes to God but through the Queer." If you know me, you will know God. From now on just know that you know God, because I, the Queer, am standing right in front of you."

Phillip declared, "Show us God and we will be satisfied." The Queer replied, "I have been with you the whole time. Phillip you still don't know me? Whoever has seen the Queer has seen God. Do you believe in me or not? I only speak the words of the God that sent me. I and God are one. All who believe in the Queer, will emulate the works of the Queer. If you ask anything in my name, the Queer, I will do it."

"If you love all of me, every identity, sexuality, orientation, ability, and race embodied in me, you will keep my commandment to love all people. There is another advocate coming who will be with you forever, the Spirit of Truth. The world will never be able to catch the Spirit of Truth, because no one has a monopoly on truth. You will know the Spirit when the Spirit abides in you."

"I will not leave you alone. I am coming to you and will make all things right. In a little while I will be hidden, but you will see me; because I live, you will also live. On that day you will know that the Queer is God and that God is in the Queer. The ones that keep the commandments of love and justice are the ones that really love the Queer. Those who love, I will love and reveal myself to them." Judas asked, "How is it that you will reveal yourself to us and not to the world?" The Queer replied, "Those who love me will love others. Those who love will know the Queer and I will make my home in them. Whoever does not love God or others does not keep my commandments. Slowly may all of this world learn to love. This is the word of God."

"I have told you these things while the Queer is still here. The Advocate, the Holy Spirit, who is coming as God will remind you of the words of the Queer. Peace I leave with you, my peace, a peace that affirms the queer in all persons without qualification, I give you. I do not give noramilization and security as the world gives. I give you a peace to be who you are. Do not be afraid, and do not let anyone else be afraid. I am going away. If you love me, you will rejoice for a higher love is coming. I will reveal such love to you. Believe. I will not talk much more. I am growing tired and depressed.

Evil is all around, but it has no power. I make my own decisions. I do what I am about to do so that the world will know God through the Queer. Get up, let's go."

Chapter 15

"I am the electricity of life and God is the source of life. Those who are walking around dead need to connect with the electricity of life. You have been given tremendous cleansing electricity through the words of the Queer. Live in me and I will live in you. Your life will have no electricity without me. You will give electricity to others if you stay connected to me. Whoever does not stay connected to me, will have no electricity and power to live. If you have my electricity you will be able to change the world. The Queer will give you anything you need. God is glorified by the Queer. As God loves you, so do I. As I love you, so does God. Keep my commandments and abide in love, just as I have abided in the love of God. I want to restore your life."

"This is my desire, that you love one another as I have loved you. This is the queerest action of the Queer, sacrificial love. No one has greater love than the one who lays down their life for all. You are my friends. I call you friends, because all has been made known to you. I am out. I am proud. I am the Queer. You don't have to choose me, because I have already chosen you. I appointed you to love each other, so that God will be glorified and the world might be put to right. I, the Queer, am giving you all of these teachings so that you might love each other and restore love."

"If the world hates you, be aware that it hated me for my queerness. If you belong to the world and normalize yourself, doing exactly what the world says, then the world will love you as its own. But when you come out, the world tries to break you into conformity. I have chosen all to be queer just like me, and the world hates all things queer. Queerness is from God. Remember the word I, the Queer gave you, 'If they persecuted me they are going to persecute you. Phobias are rampant. The hate crimes, bullying, violence, and derision that you experience is that same hate crimes, bullying, violence, and derision that I experience. I am with you always in these things. Never forget, queerness is from God. Those who commit atrocities might name God, but they do not know the God who is the source of all love and queerness. If I had not come and spoken against such bigotry and lunacy, they could plead the excuse of ignorance. Now, the Queer God has spoken and they are without excuse. Whoever hates the Queer hates God. Whoever hates my queer ones hates God. Folks have seen love and justice flow out. Unfortunately they don't follow it, they like oppression and hate more. This fulfills prophecy, 'they hate without cause.'"

"The Advocate of God will remind everyone to embrace queerness as from God and to seek love and justice above all things. You are to testify about these things to all people everywhere. Tell them that the Queer lives."

Chapter 16

"I have said all of these things to keep you queer and to not let you slip into the evil of normativity. They are going to put all of you out of the church. Unfortunately, when they kick you, the Body of the Queer, out then they actually won't be having church any longer. You will be oppressed and persecuted by religious bigots who think that they are doing the work of God by trampling on your queerness. Never listen to them. They are tools of evil. They do not know the Queer or God. I say these things so that you might have strength in the hours of trial. Stay strong in your queerness and know that God is Queer."

"I did not share the full extent of my queerness with you in the beginning, because I was with you and I prayed you might figure it out. Now, I am going back to the God that sent me here, yet none of you asks me more questions? I know you are sad and confused. I can only tell you the truth. I am not going away, the Advocate will come. When the Holy Spirit arrives the Spirit will immediately get to work on spreading justice, love, and restoration throughout the world so that evil might be overcome and defeated. Justice, because the world is oppressive and the marginalized are always mistreated. Love, because it is the only force powerful enough to turn enemies into friends. Restoration, because the world needs to be put back together again. Evil will no longer rule this world!"

"I can't bear to say too much more right now. When the Spirit comes, she will guide you in all truth; for she will speak the words of God; and she will tell of the coming restoration. She will glorify me and I her. All that God is and will ever be belongs to me. For this reason I can tell you that we are God and that we are declaring all things to you."

"I will be with you for a short time longer and then after a short time longer you will see me again." The disciples' heads were spinning in confusion, "What is the Queer talking about? How long is a little while? Where is the Queer going?" The Queer heard the murmurings and replied, "You could just ask me. You will weep for a short time and then experience ecstasy. The world is about is about to rejoice. Like a woman in full on labor, the pain lasts until the joy of the child's arrival. You have pain at this time, but joy is coming quickly. No one will take the ecstasy away from you that is coming. Why haven't you asked anything in the name of the Queer? Ask and you will get it."

"I know that I have used a lot of figures of speech, but you will understand these things by and by. The hour is coming when you will see all things plainly. On that day you will ask anything in the name of the Queer and God will give it, because God is the Queer and the Queer is God. God loves you and that is why God sent me. I came from God and I am going to God."

The disciples rejoiced, "Finally! The Queer is speaking plainly. Now we don't have any further questions and we know for sure that the Queer has come from God." The Queer answered them, "You believe now? You are about to scatter and desert me. Yet, I am never alone, as God is always in me. These are words of peace. In this world you will deal with some real shit, but have strength and courage, I have conquered the world with love."

Chapter 17

After the Queer spoke these words, the Queer looked up to heaven and said, "The hour for the murderous hate crime has come. Glorify the Queer that the Queer might glorify you. I know that you have given all authority to me to give eternal life to all people. These events are so that all people might know that you are the one true God and I am your one true Queer. I am finishing the work that you gave me to do, I love them in spite of the hate crime that is coming. So, now God glorify the Queer with the glory that I had before the creation of the universe."

"I have made your name known to all people. They are your people, you have granted them to me, and they have kept and are learning to keep your word. Now

The Queer

know that the Queer's word is your word. They know the truth that flows from God. I asking for your justice and love on their behalf. I am asking for all of your children. All my children are your children and all your children are my children. I am glorified in them. Now, the Queer is no longer in the world, but the queer children remain in the world. I am coming straight to you. God make them one, so that they might love each other and create peace and love together. I have always tried to protect them. I made sure that not one would be lost. But now my work is done, I speak all of this so that the world may know what is happening and have joy. I, the Queer, have given them your word. The world hates them, because they are queer too and do not belong to the world, just as I am queer and do not belong to the world. I am not asking you to take them out of the world, just make them safe from hate, bigotry, and oppression within it. Protect them from evil. They are queer just like me, keep them safe God. Fill them with truth, fill them with your word of love. As you have sent the Queer into the world, so too have I sent all the queers out into the world. I go through with this, so that they might know what love looks like. May this example of love sanctify them in truth."

"I ask for all people who are here and are to come, that they may all be one. I want them to be just like us, God is in the Queer and the Queer is in God. I want the world to know that I am the God sent to earth. The glory you grant me, I give to them so that they may be unified as one. I love them as you have loved me. God let all people be with the Queer constantly, let them know my presence through my love for them. These are my people and have been my people before the foundation of the world."

"Holy God, the world is often blinded to your presence, but I am not. I know queerness and my followers know the Queer. They know me. I made your name known to them, Queer. I will make it known unto the ends of the earth so

The Queer

that all might love the queerness within and the queerness without. The love that you have loved me with, I want that love to be in all of them. The Queer will exist in all of them, forever."

Chapter 18

After the Queer spoke all of these words, the time of darkness was rapidly approaching, the Queer and the disciples cruised down to a solitary garden within Quakertown Park. Judas knew the place, as he and the Queer had been there before. Suddenly, without much warning, sirens and spotlights filled the place. Some of the police cars jumped curbs and almost rammed some of the disciples. The police jumped out of their cars with guns drawn, "Freeze you queers! If anyone makes a move you will die." The sergeant with the police officer remarked, "What in the hell are all of these different types of people doing together in Quakertown Park in the middle of the night? Straights, blacks, whites, Hispanics, Asians, Native Americans, gays, lesbians, bisexual, transgender, pansexual, intersexual, women, men, and all kinds of folks. I haven't seen this type of diversity since I worked for Fort Worth and participated in the raid on the Rainbow Lounge. Are ya'll planning the world's most diverse orgy imaginable? Who are we hear to get? " "The Queer," one of the rookie officers replied. "Judas, do your thing," whispered the sergeant. Before Judas could act, the Queer exclaimed, "Who are you looking for?" They all answered, "The Queer from Ponder." The Queer replied, "That's me." Judas was standing right next to the Queer. When the Queer answered the question, every race, sexuality, class, and identity fell to the ground. Again the Queer asked, "Who are you looking for?" They again replied, "The Queer from Ponder." "I told you that is me! If you are looking for me, then let all of these other folks go," the Queer replied. The Queer did not lose a single one of the disciples. Then Peter pulled out a pistol and shot Malchus, the assistant to the pastor at the Church of the Bible. The blast missed everything vital, but blew Malchus' right ear clean off. The Queer promptly healed Malchus' ear and looked to Peter, "Don't ever use a gun again. My people have no use for guns. Those who carry guns will die by guns. Am I not supposed to do what I have been called to do? Are you not supposed to do what God has called you to do? How can you love anyone holding a gun? Take me away officers!"

So the police officers arrested the Queer and bound the Queer with plastic zip ties. First, they took the Queer to the pastor of the Church in the Village, a queerphobic underling of the pastor of the Church of the Bible. The pastor of the Church of the Bible had told all who would listen that is was time to arrest and execute the Queer. It was better for one to die than queerness be rampant in Denton.

Peter and another disciple followed the squad cars carrying the Queer to the Church in the Village. Upon arrival, since people were familiar with the disciples, Peter and the other disciple kept their distance and looked in the windows of the Church in the Village to watch what was happening. Ultimately, they both decided to go to the outskirts of the sanctuary. A woman who was at the Church in the Village all the time approached Peter and declared, "Are you not one of the disciples of the Queer? Are you queer yourself?" Peter lied and said, "I am not." Rather than following the Queer, the closet seemed a much safer space at the moment. Peter walked over to a television showing a basketball game, where the police officers and some staff of the church were gathered, and tried to breath for a moment.

The pastor of the Church in the Village questioned the Queer in the large sanctuary about the disciples and the teachings. The questioning was on large screens for the entire quickly gathered congregation to see. As the questioning commenced, dramatic guitar chords played over the loud speakers. It was a typical service at the Church in the Village, except that someone's life was at stake. The Queer responded to the questioning, "I have been honest, I have taught in all types of churches. I have never been closeted with any of my teachings. Why do you ask? You have ears. You have heard my teachings." One of the nearby police officers struck the Queer in the face and screamed, "Is this how you address the pastor of the Church in the Village?" The gathered congregation cheered and screamed for more blood. All the components of a hate crime were in place. The Queer spewed blood and managed, "I have not lied, so why do you strike me?" To the disappointment of the gathered, who wanted to see an execution right now, the pastor of the Church in the Village sent the Queer to the pastor of the Church of the Bible.

Peter was still watching the basketball game with the officers and church staff when one of the officers looked at him and said, "Weren't you with the Queer earlier?" Peter snapped back, "I am not queer and I don't know the Queer." One of the cousins of Malchus, whose ear Peter shot off, saw Peter and said, "I saw you in Quakertown Park!" Peter shuttered and said, "It was not me!" At that instance, a dog outside of the church barked three times.

Once the pastor of the Church of the Bible got hold of the Queer, he took the Queer immediately to the residence of Pilate, the Mayor of Denton. The mob of religious folks had guns and banged on the door of the Mayor's residence demanding she come out. "We values voters put you in office and we can take you out in a minute," they screamed. So Pilate came out on the porch and inquired, "What accusations have you brought against this Queer?" The religious folk screamed in unison, "If this where not a criminal then why would we bring the Queer to you?" Pilate responded, "Take the Queer and judge the Queer based on your laws and your interpretations. That is what you usually do anyways." The religious folk snapped back, "Unfortunately, our laws and interpretations do not allow us to put someone to death."

Pilate entered her house with the Queer and asked the Queer, "Are you the Queer of God?" "Do you ask this because you believe or because others made you?" the Queer responded. "I am not religious and frankly I don't give a shit, but those folks out there can run me out of office. Your own religious folks turned you over to me. What exactly have you done?" replied Pilate. The Queer answered, "I am queer and in this world that is enough to get you killed. I am not from here. I am from God. No one is fighting my attackers, because they know that death cannot hold me. My queerness is not of this world. I am the Queer of God." Pilate responded, "So, you are a governor, bishop, or president of some other world?" The Queer replied, "I am the Queer and for this I have come from God. I came to earth to die for the queerness of all people. I came to earth because I love all people. I was born for this very moment to testify to the truth of love. Everyone who cares about love listens to my voice." Pilate responded fleetingly as she whipped around to go back out on the porch, "What the fuck is truth?" "The queerness of love and individuality," the Queer managed to whisper.

When Pilate arrived outside, she went to the pastor of the Church of the Bible and said, "I find no fault in this Queer...but I have a tradition that the religious folks in town pardon a criminal once a year. Do you want me to release the Queer of God?" The crowd shouted with blood curtailing shrieks, "Kill the Queer, release Barabbas." Now, Barabbas killed a local family for sport earlier in the year. This shows the hatred the folks carried for queerness and the Queer.

Chapter 19

Pilate had the Queer tortured in the city jail in hopes that torture might satisfy the blood lust of the religious mob and leadership. The police officers wove a crown of glow sticks and aluminum cans and shoved it down into the flesh of the Queer's head. They took a broomstick and shoved it up the Queer's anus. The officers mutilated the Queer's genitalia by stabbing it with paper clips. As if all of that was not enough, they placed the Queer in a burning barrel and lit the Queer on fire using lighter fluid. When they finished with the torture, the officers took a rainbow robe and put it on the Queer. The officers kept coming up to the Queer, saying, "All hail the Queer of God!" and each time they took turns peeing on the Queer. The officers also struck the Queer on the face as often as they could. Pilate went to the jail and asked for the torture to stop. She told the religious folk, "I am bringing the Queer out to you to see the punishment I ordered and that there is now no further fault in the Queer." So the Queer came out, wearing the crown of glow sticks and aluminum cans and the rainbow robe, to face the crowd, which now had swelled to a couple thousand people. Pilate said, "Here is the Queer." When the pastor of the Church of the Bible saw the Queer, he led the chorus of voices, "Kill the Queer! Kill the Queer! Kill the Queer!" Pilate declared, "Take the Queer and do it yourselves, I find no fault in the Queer." The religious folk screamed, "Leviticus says that we should kill the Queer and that is what we intend to do."

When Pilate heard this, she was more afraid than ever. Pilate knew that if she didn't do what they say then she would lose her job and perhaps even be killed by the mob herself. In her house, she again asked the Queer, "Where are you from?" The Queer refused to answer any more questions. Pilate grew frustrated, "How can you refuse to answer my questions? Your life is on the line." The Queer responded, "You have no power over me. I am giving my life. The religious folks have the responsibility." From then on Pilate tried to let the Queer go, but the religious folk cried out, "If you release the Queer, you are no friend of the Governor of Texas. Everyone who claims to be from God is saying that they have higher standing than our Governor. This is just not possible!"

When Pilate heard these words, she brought the Queer into a courtroom at the Denton County Courthouse. The time was about noon. Then Pilate began to administer the death penalty as it is usually administered in Texas, swiftly with little regard for facts. Pilate asked the religious folk, who served as the jury, "What do you want to do?" They all shouted in unison, "Kill the Queer! Kill the Queer! Kill the Queer!" The courtroom erupted. Pilate screamed over the melee, "So, your verdict is death." They all screamed, "Yes." The religious folk seized the Queer with the pastor of the Church of the Bible leading the way. The state-approved hate crime continued.

They forced the Queer to walk the streets of the town as they shouted, "Kill the Queer! Kill the Queer! Kill the Queer!" The Queer carried a cross that was painted purple. Finally, after several beatings in alleys, public bathrooms, and small parks, they took the Queer to the Denton Square. There they nailed the Queer's hands and feet until blood dripped onto the stark green lawn. There were two other crucified next to the Queer, they had committed religious crimes as well, one denied the inerrancy of scripture and the other declared all people bound for heaven. The Queer was right in the middle. Pilate had the inscription "The Queer" written in English and Spanish on a board and placed on the cross over the Queer's head. Many of the religious folk read the inscription and asked that it be changed, because they were afraid of federal hate crime statutes. Pilate answered, "What is written is written, just put your trust in your bigoted religion." When the police officers helped the religious folk crucify the Queer, they took the Queer's clothes and divided them amongst each other. There was a shiny purple silk shirt that a couple of officers wanted, so they rolled dice to see who got it. As one of the officers won, a sharp sound of agony came from the Queer.

Meanwhile, standing near the Queer's cross, was Mary, the Queer's Mother, her sister Mary, and Mary Magdalene. When the Queer saw the Queer's mother and John, the Queer declared, "I am your son." Then the Queer said to John, "She is your mother." John knew that this meant that he was to take care of the Queer's mother, for the Queer adored the Queer's mother.

After this, the Queer knew that time was drawing to a close, the Queer said, "Can I at least have something to drink before I die?" The officers couldn't resist one last bout of torture. They filled a sponge on a stick with their urine and sent it up the Queer. When the Queer smelled the urine, the Queer refused it, and declared, "I am finished." The Queer bowed the Queer's head and died. The thousands of religious folk in attendance and the many religious folk watching live on local television cheered. The pastor of the Church of the Bible slapped hands with the pastor of the Church in the Village and said, "We have finally killed that inclusive queer shit!"

The other two victims on their crosses were still alive and asked for mercy. The officers shot them both in the head. "That will teach them to question the inerrancy of the Bible and the limited nature of heaven," declared the pastor of the Church in the Village. When the officers checked the Queer again, they realized the Queer was dead, one exceedingly queerphobic officer took a gun with a bayonet attached and shoved it into the side of the Queer. Blood and water poured out the side of the Queer. The wound fulfilled ancient prophesy of a last queerphobic wound and identified the Queer as the true Queer of God.

After all these events, a secret disciple of the Queer, Joseph of Krum, asked Pilate to be allowed to bury the Queer in a private cemetery in Fred Moore Park. Pilate agreed and the body was taken to the cemetery. Nicodemus, who first came to the Queer in secret, also came and financially made sure that the body of the Queer was properly embalmed. They took the body of the Queer and placed the Queer in an all white outfit. On top of the casket was a rainbow flag, representing the rainbow peoples of the world the Queer loved so much. In the private cemetery there was a garden, amidst the flowers they buried the Queer with just a few people present, as most lovers of the Queer were scared that they too were going to be the next buried.

Chapter 20

Early on Sunday, while it was still dark, Mary Magdalene set out for the grave of the Queer. She didn't live too far away and thought the early morning walk would be good to calm her nerves. When Mary Magdalene arrived, she noticed that the ground was moved and the coffin was open. Completely unnerved, Mary Magdalene ran to the other side of town, were the disciples were hiding, to tell Peter and John. "They have taken my Queer, and I don't know where they have laid my Queer!" she managed to blurt out exasperated. Peter and John took off toward Fred Moore Park. John outran Peter and saw the open empty coffin. Looking in, John noticed the Queer's white clothes lying there folded. Peter ran up, diving into the coffin, Peter screamed, "Where is the Queer?" John got into the coffin as well and believed something supernatural was happening. The disciples returned to the hideout confused about what was actually going on.

Mary Magdalene stayed crying at the tomb, for she really loved the Queer. Feeling as if someone was watching her, she looked up and there were two angels standing at the coffin. They asked, "Why are you crying?" Mary Magdalene managed, "They have taken my Queer, and I don't know where they have laid my Queer." When she said this, she turned around and saw another familiar looking figure standing there. The figure asked, "Why are you crying? Who are you looking for?" Unable to place exactly who it was and thinking it might be the gardener, Mary Magdalene answered, "Sir, if you know where the Queer is, just tell me." "Mary," replied the Queer affectionately. "Holy Shit!" replied Mary. "Don't grab at me. I have not yet ascended to God. Go to the disciples and tell them I am ascending to our God," remarked the

Queer. Mary Magdalene ran to the disciples and shouted, "I have seen the Queer!"

Later on in the evening, with the doors locked for fear of the religious folks, the Queer walked through the wall and said, "Peace!" After exchanging greetings, the Queer showed them the wounds. Then, and only after seeing the wounds, the disciples believed and rejoiced. The Queer declared, "I send you to share love and your wounds with others. After saying this, the Queer breathed the Holy Spirit onto them, "Receive the Spirit. Go and love. Forgive and speak of forgiveness. Bless the people and be a blessing."

Thomas was not present when the Queer showed up. So the other disciples told her what happened. "We have seen the Queer!" they declared. Thomas couldn't believe it and remarked, "Unless I put my finger where the nail pierced, see where the glow sticks and aluminum cans pierced the skull, smell the urine on the body, see the burns, and put my hand in the side, I cannot believe."

A week later, as the disciples were sharing some drinks, the Queer came through the wall and stood amongst them. "Peace friends!" greeted the Queer. Then the Queer remarked to Thomas, "Sniff the urine, ok now put your fingers in these gashes on my head, touch my legs, feel the burns, now the hands, put your fingers in the holes, and now the side, put your fist in my side. Believe Thomas." Thomas exclaimed, "You are my God!" The Queer replied, "You have believed because you have touched. Blessed are those who believe because they have learned to feel."

The Queer did many signs and wonders in this place. Description of all the beauty that took place in Denton and elsewhere during this time could not be contained in a million books. The present description is written so that you might know the depth and height of the love the Queer has for you, believe that the

The Queer

Queer is the child of God sent to save you and the rest of the world, and trust that, like the Queer, you can use your wounds to find life in yourself and give life to others. Life flows from the Queer.

Chapter 21

A short time after all of this magic, the Queer appeared again to the disciples at Lake Ray Roberts. The sighting happened in this way. Peter and six other disciples were all out on a camping trip and trying to get some rest away from the fears of Denton. Late one night, Peter declared, "I'm going fishing!" Everybody else declared, "We're going too!" They all loved going out fishing and spending the night on the boat. They had a few cans of beer and were having a pretty good time, but didn't catch anything.

Right after the sun came up, the disciples looked up and a familiar looking person was standing on the shore. They didn't know it was the Queer. "Friends, have

The Queer

you caught any fish?" remarked the Queer. They replied with a resounding, amused, and emphatic, "No!" The Queer said, "Well, put all the poles you have into the water right now." They did as they were told. Then fish started hitting the poles and jumping into the boat. There were fish going everywhere. The disciples were worried the boat was going to sink and grew frightened. John then recognized the familiar figure and remarked to Peter, "It is the Queer." Peter couldn't contain himself and dove into the water as he was putting his bathing suit on. Swimming as fast as he possible could, Peter couldn't wait to reach the Queer. The other disciples were trying to get the boat and fish to shore.

Once they arrived, then went and sat down next to the Queer and a charcoal fire. The Queer was cooking some fish and bread. "Fresh fish is my favorite," remarked the Queer. Peter helped put everything together. The Queer asked, "Is everybody ready for breakfast?" No one spoke, they were all just in awe of the presence of the Queer. They all ate breakfast and felt completely whole in the presence of the Queer.

This was the third post-mortem appearance of the Queer.

After breakfast, the Queer said to Peter, "Do you love me?" Peter replied, "Yes, you know that I love you." The Queer replied, "Feed my people the bread of life." A second time the Queer asked Peter, "Do you love me?" Peter growing frustrated, "You know that I love you." The Queer replied, "Take care of my people by sharing your wounds and healing the wounds of others." A third time the Queer asked Peter, "Do you love me?" Peter was hurt and replied, "You know everything and you know that I love you." The Queer replied, "Feed the people the sustenance of love. No matter your strength, ability, or level of belief, just follow me."

Peter turned and saw John had snuck up behind them to be close to the Queer and to eavesdrop. "What happens to that guy?" Peter jealously remarked. The Queer sharply responded, "What difference should that make to you? I will deal with him however I want. You, keep your eyes on me." The disciples learned much in this time about caring for themselves while not wasting time on negative thoughts about others.

We know that the words and testimony contained in this book are true, for the disciple who has written them has actually walked with the Queer. However, one must never forget that world cannot contain all the things that the Queer has done.

The Queer of Ponder is Jesus of Nazareth.

www.ingramcontent.com/pod-product-compliance
Lightning Source LLC
Chambersburg PA
CBHW070926160426
43193CB00011B/1588